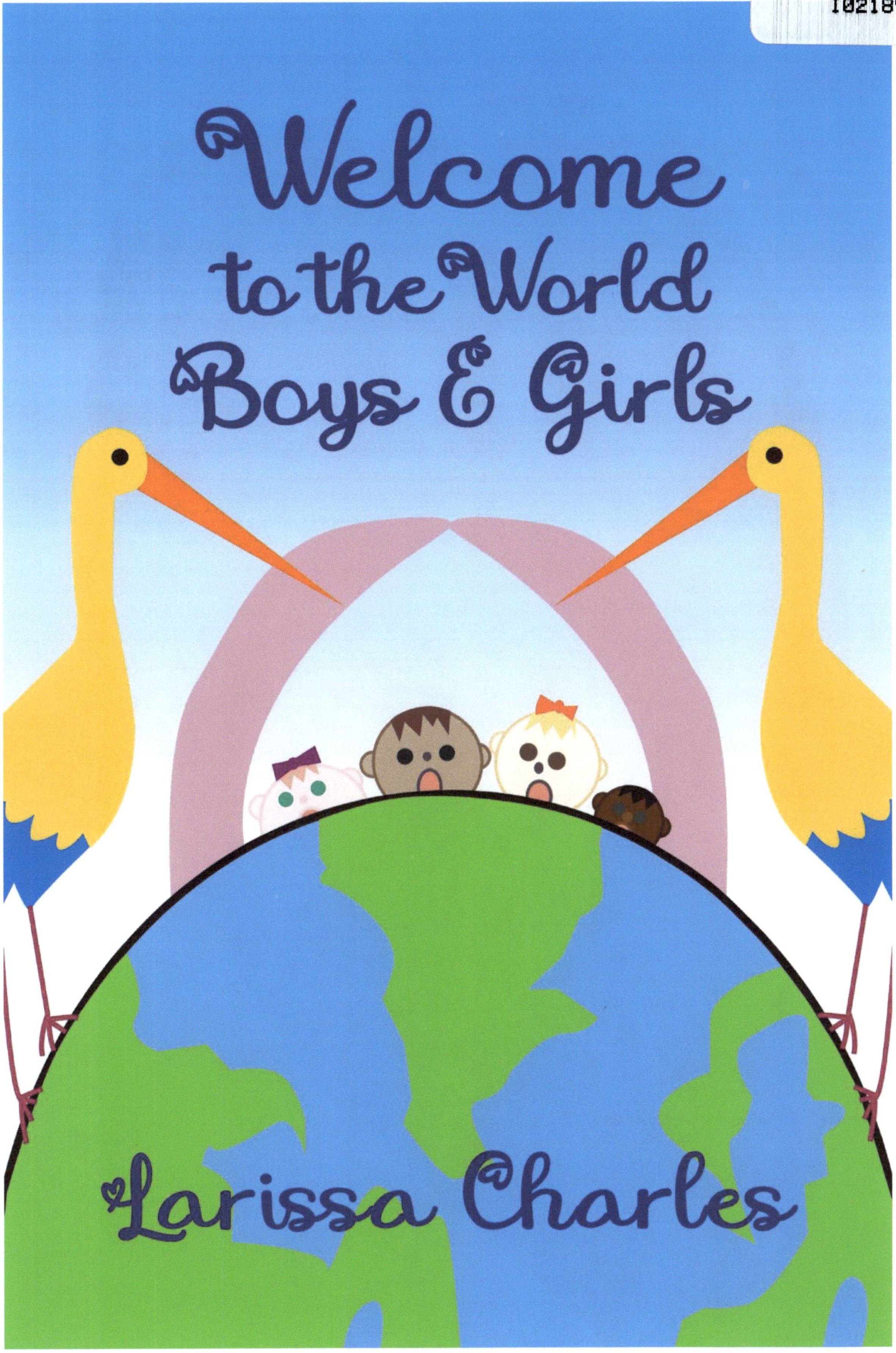

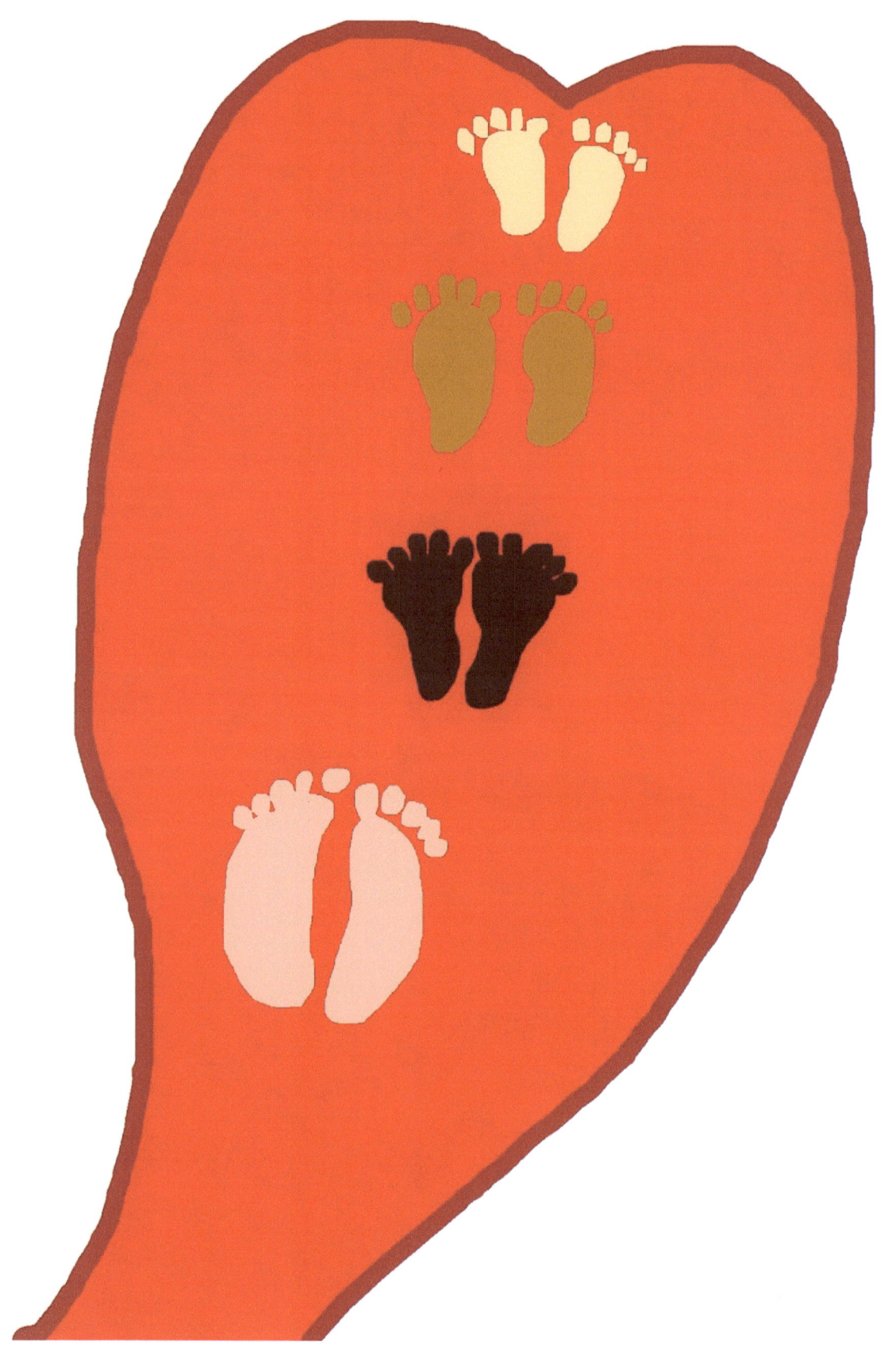

Welcome to the World Boys and Girls!

Written and Illustrated
By
Larissa Charles

Book Design
By
Joleene Naylor

© Copyright 2020 by Larissa Charles.

This book is dedicated to Hayden and all the newborn babies in the world.

Welcome to the world boys and girls.

There's something beautiful everywhere you turn.

When you first open your eyes, it is the bright light you see.

And then you meet your mummy and daddy.

You give them so much joy and happiness that you make their hearts dance.

They carry you into thier arms and give you all the warmth and life's every chance.

And that's how you know how much you are loved.

To your nursery you are taken and made comfortable and cosy.

In there you sleep soundly for many hours after your feed.

You get used to wearing clothes such as mittens, hats and onsies.

But there is nothing more comforting than your snuggly, wuggly blanky.

You gaze at your favourite adults and then begin to smile. You reach out for your mobiles with so much delight.

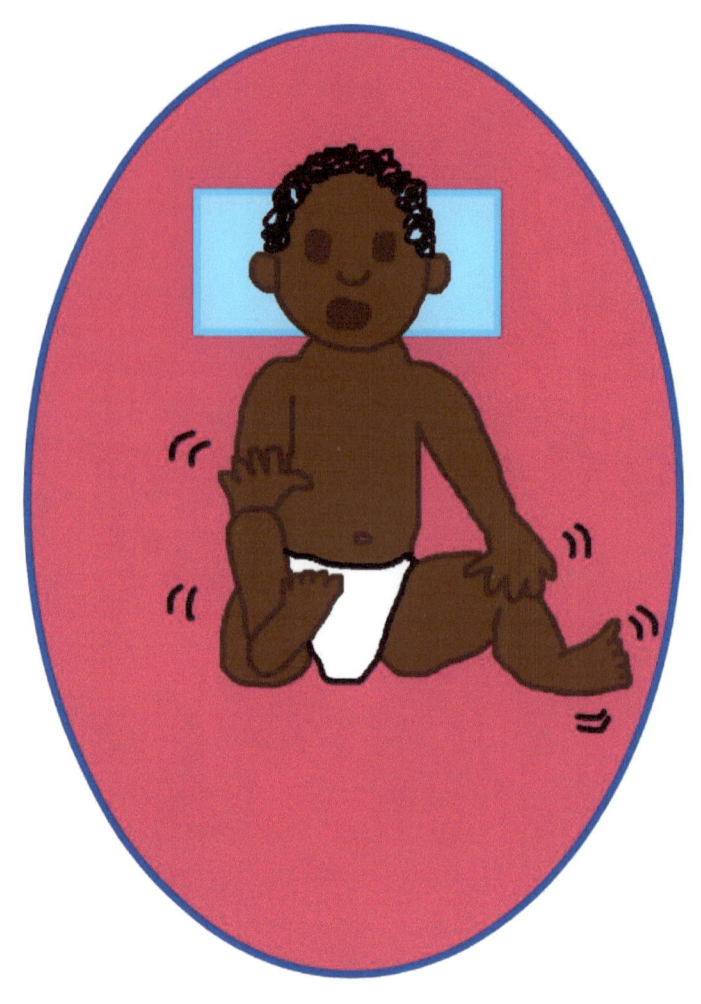

You love to wriggle your body, your little fingers and your toes. Sometimes you even try to twitch your little nose.

Every now and then, you need to get some fresh air. So, you are put in a buggy and taken everywhere.

You have so much awaiting you. Little by little you will see and discover all the wonders in store for thee.

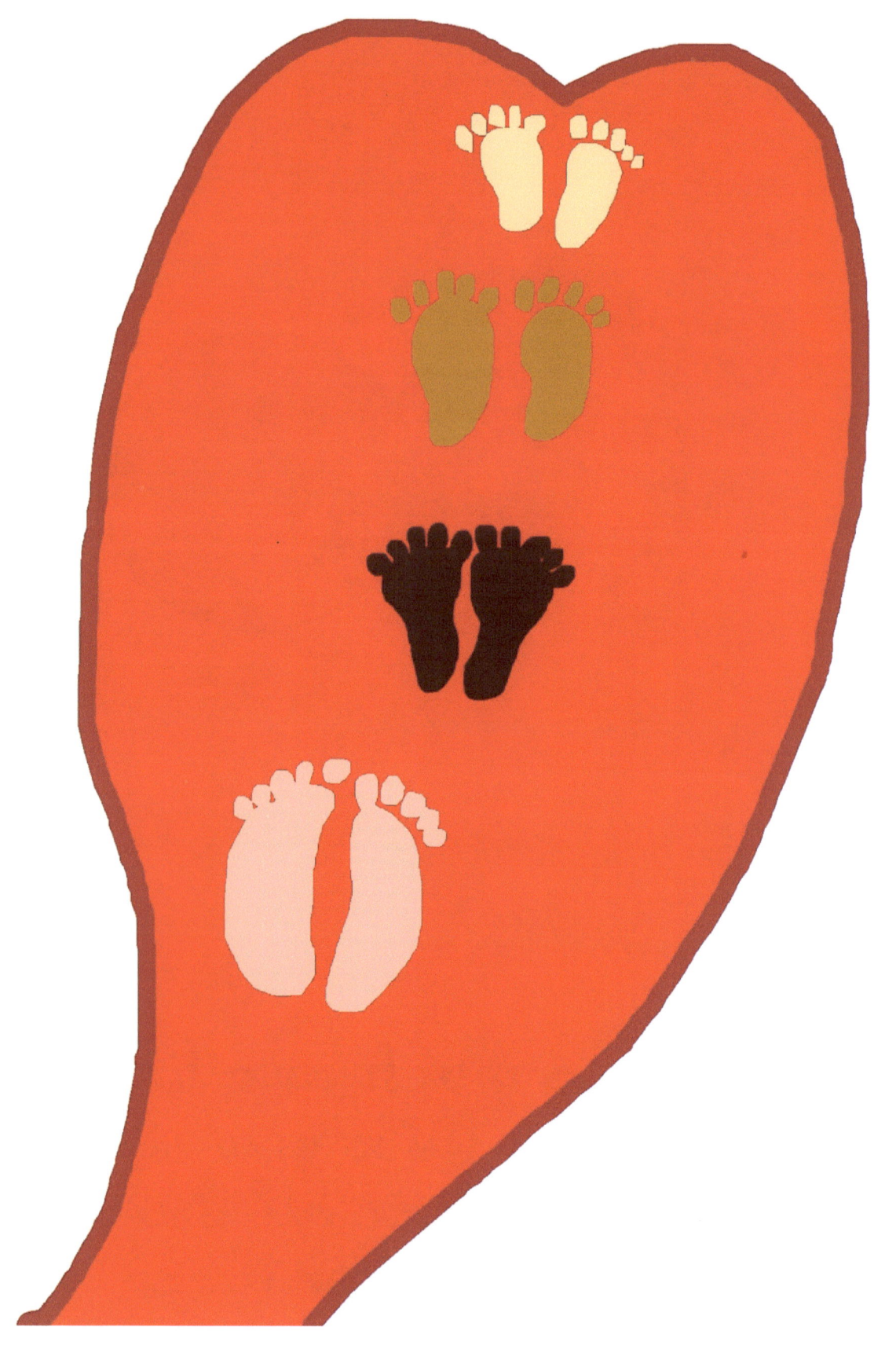

www.ingramcontent.com/pod-product-compliance
Lightning Source LLC
Chambersburg PA
CBHW041234040426
42444CB00002B/160